Spirituality

D0525137

Make God Your Friend

Carol Williams

Introduction by Rosalind Rinker

ZONDERVAN
PUBLISHING HOUSE

OF THE ZONDERVAN CORPORATION
GRAND RAPIDS, MICHIGAN 49506

MAKE GOD YOUR FRIEND

© 1975 by The Zondervan Corporation
Grand Rapids, Michigan

Second printing May 1975

Library of Congress Catalog Card Number: 74-25343

Printed in the United States of America.

In memory of my father
RALPH M. WILLIAMS
who with love and by
example helped me to
make God my friend.

Contents

Foreword

People often thank me for the simple, rhythmic style of my writing, but it involves more than appears on the surface.

I give God thanks for the gift He has given me, but I have the author of this book to thank for the long, difficult sessions she endured with me as editor of my books, *You Can Witness with Confidence* and *Communicating Love Through Prayer*.

These editorial encounters were exhausting for both of us — a real trial to test the measure and depth of friendship. Our friendship did survive, however, and these books are now on my best seller list.

Carol's approach differs from mine, but *Make God Your Friend* is a book that I recommend you read and give to a friend or acquaintance who refuses to read most evangelical literature. It will give you both new insights.

Make God Your Friend is keyed for those still seeking to give their lives a meaningful sense of coordination.

The language, illustrations, reasons, and persuasions in this book are especially designed for those who have experienced painful encounters with well-intentioned but overzealous Christians. It is short, terse, and to-the-point.

If you want to be turned-on to a new spiritual approach, I urge you to read this book. I predict you will think of many with whom you will want to — will feel impelled to — share it.

ROSALIND RINKER

Preface

Many who admit that God is the Creator of the universe conceive of Him as being a power so distant and remote from their affairs and concerns that they find it virtually impossible to communicate with Him.

If we are to know God loves us, then we must be willing to converse with Him. We do this through prayer.

When our prayer communication is comfortable and natural, it becomes the two-way communication God intends it to be. It enables us to know that God does speak to us and that He is our friend.

It is hoped this small volume will open a new and exciting adventure for those who have not yet made God their friend.

1

How Do
You Pray?

"God, Christ, faith, prayer, and all such nonsense serve merely as opiates for fear-ridden, superstitious idiots!"

I stared in fascination at the table where my friend was nervously making wet circles with the bottom of his glass.

I waited for him to continue his tirade, but when silence followed I said, "Dick, you are a fine writer. You are also a meticulous grammarian. Furthermore, you take pride in having an excellent vocabulary. But I wonder if you realize that you are unable to speak more than two sentences without emphasizing what you say by taking God's name in vain?"

His dark eyes looked a bit startled as he replied, "Really? I've never noticed."

"You have," I said, "a most vitriolic tongue even when you are not discussing religion. As a matter of fact, you can be downright insulting when you choose to be. You consign most people to a realm of sheer idiocy. Yet hasn't it ever seemed strange to you that more often than not you seem to want to talk about religion when we are together?

"It strikes me," I continued, "that while you take a totally negative attitude on this particular subject, it still seems to nag and gnaw at you. Haven't you ever wondered why?"

He frowned at his half-empty glass, and I watched his expression become unpleasant, apparently stirred by some bitter memory.

After a pause he said, "When I was a little boy, I had to live with an aunt I hated. Each Sunday she dragged me to church in her pompous, supercilious, sanctimonious way. One Sunday when I was twelve, I exploded with anger as we were coming home from church. I swore angrily. It really rocked the old gal — just as I knew it would. She stiffened and said, 'Richard! If you ever again say that, God will strike you dead!' We glared at each other the rest of the way home. As soon as I could escape her clutches, do you know what I did?"

"No, what did you do?"

"I ran. Almost a mile. To the edge of the city dump near her home. At the edge of it I stood for a moment, then shouted across it — over and over — the oath I had used that morning. And guess what happened?"

"What happened, Dick?"

"Nothing! Absolutely nothing! As you can see, God did not strike me dead as that pseudopious old bat assured me He would."

For a long moment silence hung between us. Then I said, "No, God did not strike you dead physically. But I suspect something within you died."

Apparently my answer was not quite what he expected, for he made no reply. Instead he stared moodily at the contents of his glass.

"Dick, you're like a man driven by something beyond his control. We both know what was once only a cocktail has turned into a drinking problem you cannot manage. It has affected not only you but your work and your family. You make a good living, yes. But you are plagued with tensions, doubts, and debts. You're bitter about your wife's mental illness. You're angry at the psychiatrists. In fact, you seem angry at the whole world. Yet always, whether in anger or in ordinary conversation, you have an almost unconscious compulsion to punctuate your speech by taking God's name in vain."

Before he could reply, I added, "Look, Dick, I'm not your aunt! I'm truly sorry about the pain she caused you. But you are no longer a child. You are a grown man. A sensitive, talented man. Also an unhappy man. Things will never be quite right in your life until you decide to seek God as a friend instead of waging your own vituperative war against Him as your supposed enemy."

Defensively he replied, "I don't need God." Then hastily added, "Besides, I don't believe there is a God. And even if I did want to believe, I wouldn't know how — let alone know how to pray."

How to pray?

getting started — that causes us the most difficulty.

It is impossible for us to pray without using our minds. It also is impossible for us to pray without using words or feelings, either silently or audibly.

If we feel uncomfortable with our choice of words because they seem stilted and unfamiliar, then we are in trouble before we have really begun.

To many of us, the ecclesiastical pronouns *Thou, Thee,* and *Thy* appear strangely distant and formal. If this be the case, then we need have no compunction about dropping them from use in our prayers.

> The high English (you, me, yours) was used for the royal family, nobility and for special ceremonies. The low English (thou, thee, thy) was used in the home, intimately with the family, and in addressing God.
>
> As time went on this usage was reversed. The forms used for royalty became everyday family terms and today we all say you, me, yours. However, the old terms persisted with the Quakers at all times, and with the religious people at church and at prayer. The King James Bible was translated into English during the Shakespearean period, and so the low form, the familiar endearing family terms were used: thy, thou, thee. And they have come down to us today in our English Bible and in our religious services. The original languages from which our English Bible came to us make no such distinction.[1]

Here you may well say, "But you are assuming I already pray when I don't."

Fair enough! So let's assume you added, "As a matter of fact, I'm not even sure there is a God. Or maybe, as so many said not long ago, God is dead.

[1] Rosalind Rinker, *Prayer — Conversing with God* (Grand Rapids: Zondervan Publishing House, 1959), p. 22.

So how can I possibly pray to a deity who might not exist?"

If you're going to ask me to define God for you, I can't. God is spirit and, as such, is beyond the stricture of human definition.

But to use an analogy: Neither of us actually sees the flow of electricity, yet each of us sees its manifestation in our home. We accept it, and we use it.

Neither of us can actually see the human spirit either. But we certainly do see it manifested for either good or for evil.

The phrases "team spirit," "get in the spirit of things," "the Christmas spirit," or "come on, lift your spirit out of the doldrums," have become, like equally familiar expressions, part of our vocabulary. I doubt that you have seriously questioned them. You obviously don't actually see — and don't expect to see — the spirit itself. But you certainly do see the manifestations of it.

Jesus repeatedly said that what He did was not done by Himself but by God the Father through Him. Even as God worked through Christ, so He works through the "spirit" in each of us.

I said I could not define God. However, Christ did this for us when He said, "God is a Spirit: and they that worship him must worship him in spirit and in truth" (John 4:24, KJV). Christ also said, "I and my Father are one" (John 10:30, KJV).

Here it may help you a little to know that your doubts are no bigger or greater than those of others.

Most of us know the expression "doubting Thomas," even though not familiar with the Scripture story. However, you may not know that it was not only Thomas who doubted and questioned. The other disciples had their share of such feelings, including Philip, the fifth disciple called by Christ, for he said, "Lord, show us the Father, and we shall be satisfied" (John 14:8, RSV).

Without any irreverence intended or implied, isn't what Philip asked very much like our modern expression, "I'm from Missouri, so you'll have to prove it! Show me!"

Jesus with gentle patience answered:

> Have I been with you so long, and yet you do not know me, Philip? He who has seen me has seen the Father; how can you say, 'Show us the Father'? Do you not believe that I am in the Father and the Father in me? The words that I say to you I do not speak on my own authority; but the Father who dwells in me does his works (John 14:9, 10, RSV).

Then our Lord with infinite love, compassion, and understanding adds:

> Believe me that I am in the Father and the Father in me; or else believe me for the sake of the works themselves.
> Truly, truly, I say to you, he who believes in me, will also do the works that I do; and greater works than these will he do, because I go to the Father. Whatever you ask in my name, I will do it that the Father may be glorified in the Son; if you will ask anything in my name, I will do it (John 14:11-14, RSV).

These are wonderful, direct, and true promises.

You may still doubt that God exists, but God knows you exist.

God does speak to us in many ways, and it may startle you a bit to know that you have already responded to God, though you may have been un-aware of having done so.

If you have ever felt restless without quite knowing why — you have responded to God speaking to you.

If you have ever felt an almost overwhelming sense of beauty or have ever been profoundly aware of the sweet quality of a bird's song at twilight or dawn — then you have responded to God speaking to you.

If you have ever felt a sense of longing — you have responded to God speaking to you.

If you have ever loved — you have responded to God speaking to you.

For God is love. Divine love. Divine understanding. And God is also your friend.

When He has spoken to you, you have uncon-sciously responded. But have you ever consciously answered?

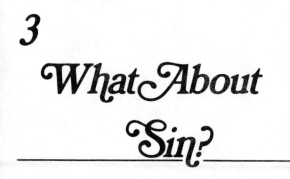

3
What About Sin?

A desire to communicate with God is the first step in our relationship with Him.

The second step involves the problem of sin, and if our prayer life is to be rich and full and meaningful, this problem must be resolved once and for all.

Often we get the sins we impose on our bodies all tangled up with the sins of our spirit or inner selves.

Our bodies are in no way sinful. God created them, and He does not create that which is evil or bad.

We have sole jurisdiction over our bodies. Excessive indulgence of any sort that involves our physical selves is not the fault of our bodies. They merely respond to our commands. Whatever the direction we set for our bodies, we are fully aware of it. We set the course. Even as the soldier who while running into enemy fire said to himself, "You have good reason to tremble, my body, knowing where I am taking you."

Each of us knows when we have exceeded the physical boundaries of right and wrong. We know, too, that we are capable of separating ourselves from good health and a sense of well-being. We know these things whether or not we are Christians. We know them whether or not we believe in God.

Unfortunately, many people, having once established for themselves criteria of right and wrong, seek arbitrarily to impose their rules of conduct on everyone they know. They consider those who do not conform to be apart from them and separated from good. In turn, the recipient of such "advice for his own good" may be thankful he feels aloof and separated from his well-intentioned advisor.

Both feel a sense of separation, and neither has helped the other to get any closer to God. Each knows something is wrong between them, but the feeling becomes worse instead of better. Most of us have experienced this at one time or another — and with it a vague sense of guilt which implies we are in some way responsible, even though we may not be able to place a mental finger on the pulse of the problem.

The term *sin* is used to connote the separation between God and man. A separation not imposed by God, but initiated by man himself.

God does not and cannot create evil. Yet we know evil exists.

Since we are aware of the existence of evil, it will help if we remember who we are — children of God, created by Him. He endowed us with minds of our own along with the power of decision: the power to accept His love for us or to reject Him and His gift of love.

When we remember this, we begin to understand, in part at least, why separation exists between God and man. But how do we span this separation?

Fortunately, God has already fully and finally resolved this problem for us. Even more, He has identified Himself with each one of us.

How? Through His beloved Son, Jesus Christ.

The deep significance of the Crucifixion is that our Lord did in fact take upon Himself the sins of each one of us — the sins of the entire world.

Many ponder Christ's words on the cross when He cried out, "My God, My God, why have You forsaken Me?" Yet He knew why. He knew that in that terrible time of separation (for God cannot be part of evil), He alone would take upon Himself the total burden of sin. That He would serve not only as our atonement but as the bridge over which all men and women may safely reach God the Father.

Jesus said, "I am the way, and the truth, and the life; no one comes to the Father, but by me" (John 14:6, RSV).

Belief in Jesus as a personal Savior is the fundamental precept of Christianity.

If you are already a Christian, you believe these words of Jesus and have already accepted Him.

If you are not a Christian, you still are probably aware of all I have just written. You simply haven't — for whatever reasons — accepted the gift of salvation.

Making this gift — which includes the "way," the "truth," and the "life" — your own isn't nearly as difficult as you may have imagined.

God has identified Himself with us through Christ. Acceptance of this is all that is required of us.

Just as God the Father is your friend and mine, so is His Son Jesus Christ our Savior and our friend.

Neither God nor Christ will ever under any circumstances fail you! The more you seek God through Christ, and the more you ask of God through Christ, the more you will receive.

The prayer of confession is our acknowledgment that we are separated from God by sin. That no matter what we do we cannot bridge this separation alone, but only through the Savior, Jesus Christ, who is our "advocate with the Father and the propitiation for our sins." In this prayer of confession we tell God our sins and ask forgiveness through Christ our Lord.

From the moment of that confession on you know you need never again be alone. You don't have to struggle alone. You can let go. You can let God.

As day by day and step by step you draw closer to God, you will find the horizons of your thought expanding and your conscience becoming more sensitive. This increased sensitivity will enable you to be more on guard against the deadly and destructive sins of the spirit. These include the sin of pride. The sin of criticizing others while patting yourself on the back because you were able to resist the temptation to which they have succumbed. Lack of humility. Feelings of smugness. I don't have to enumerate them. Your own heart will tell you — even more quickly if you ask God to jab your conscience when you have fallen into the trap of indulging them.

Don't, however, let yourself become obsessed with sin. Once you have confessed, be assured God heard you. You don't have to keep reminding Him. And God will never expect nor require of you more than you can do or give.

If you happen to fall into discouragement (and we all do now and then), get up! Start over. Don't just lie there in self-pity or delude yourself into believing you can't go on. You can! There isn't a Christian who can honestly say he has not had to start over — again — and again — and again! But with each new effort comes increased strength. Your spiritual muscles will grow as you learn not to be afraid to flex them, test them, and use them.

Every time you find a thought you know to be unworthy creeping into your mind — and this includes doubt — instantly push it out! Replace it with, "God, forgive me." Force yourself to think about Christ. Know He loves you. Know you are accepted and forgiven.

Every time you have been betrayed into rudeness or saying something cruel or unkind — immediately have the grace and humility to silently pray, "Forgive me, God." This will also help you make the first gesture of amends to the person you have injured.

Jesus specifically said, "Love your enemies, do good to those who hate you, bless those who curse you, and pray for those who treat you badly" (Luke 6:27, 28, Phillips). And He tells us that when we pray we must forgive anything we hold against another.

Here is a summary of what God expects of us:

1. A desire on our part to communicate with Him.

2. Acceptance in our minds and hearts that Jesus Christ is "the way, and the truth, and the life."

3. A willingness to confess our sins to God and a willingness to believe that through Christ our sins are forgiven forever.

4. God's promises are eternal — His truths never invalidated. But even as we are promised forgiveness, so in turn we must be willing to forgive others. We are expected to do this when we pray. In this effort God expects us to want and seek His help.

What we think about colors the entire fabric of our lives. One of the wonderful things about the Christian faith is that it provides us with a never-ending abundance of wonderful things about which to think. About which to be thankful. About which to be happy. About which to be rightfully expectant.

In attuning your thoughts to God you will not lack replacements for the thoughts you banish. All God expects of us is the courtesy of keeping our minds open and receptive to Him so that He may help us arrive at a new and deeper understanding of His love for us.

4

Not on

Your Own

I'd long debated a course of action but had, for many reasons, hesitated to take any initial step.

To a Christian friend I said, "I'll simply never be good enough to do it. To God, the very idea must appear conceited and absurd!"

My friend smiled. A gentle, understanding smile. Quietly she replied, "The day you think you are good enough to do it — don't."

So many of us seem to feel we must, through our own efforts, get our lives in order and the books balanced before we seek God's help. We tell ourselves, "One of these days I will get myself and my affairs straightened out. When I do, then I'll seek God. I'll strive to renew or strengthen my faith."

An old Chinese proverb states, "If one button on a garment is wrongly buttoned, then all the rest will go awry." And so it is in our lives when we take an initial wrong step. When we take things into our own hands. When we try the do-it-yourself method of frantically attempting to untangle the threads of discord and discontent snarling up our affairs.

As my friend knew, I had failed to include God in my planning. I had taken it upon myself to assume God would disapprove of my motive. I thought to postpone seeking His guidance until some future time when I hoped to be "good enough" to gain His approval of my objectives.

You may have made the same mistake?

Most of us would like our lives to have meaning, our work to be fruitful. We want to give and receive love, to share the blessing of friendship, to have a sense of well-being, to know the inner peace of mind which enables us to be at ease with ourselves even in the midst of outer turmoil. Yet none of us can ever achieve these things entirely on our own. When we try it, in one way or another the full measure of all we hope for eludes us — escapes us.

Our joy seems brief — our happiness fleeting.

Restlessness and discontent increasingly intrude upon us.

We become impatient and short-tempered. And as our tensions increase, so do our feelings of depression.

In seeking to recapture our dreams, resolve the problems that pressure us or the ills that plague us, we turn for help to every and any source except the One who can restore our peace of mind and get our lives back in focus.

So long as we exclude God from our thinking, planning, and action, any aid we seek will prove disappointingly inadequate. Our lives will remain discordant.

If you're tired of having your life and your thoughts cluttered with doubt, disappointment, confusion, and frustration; tired of failure; tired of unsuccessfully going-it-alone — isn't it time you stopped struggling? Isn't it time you admit you have failed in arranging your affairs without God? Isn't it time to test His love and promise to you?

How?

First, as stated in the last chapter — by a desire to seek God. Desire indicates a longing for something.

Second, by acceptance of Christ as the Way. Acceptance means to receive (something offered) with a consenting mind.

Third, by a willingness on your part to cooperate with God. The word *will* indicates purpose, choice, intention. It is power coupled with desire. It is exercising the power of your own free will.

God *is* waiting to help you. *Wants* to help you. *Will* help you — providing you do your share.

His requirements of you are threefold and direct. He asks that you love Him. Trust Him. Believe in His power to help you.

Not long ago I was talking with a friend who was seeking God as the solution to his inner turmoil. He stated he was having difficulty with this quest. Difficulty in really trusting God — even in believing in the reality of God.

I asked, "Why have you confided in me?"

"Because I trust you," he responded.

"And do you believe I am sincerely interested in how your problem is resolved?" I asked.

"Of course!" came his startled reply. "You are my friend."

I smiled. "Do you realize you have just told me that you trust me, believe in me, and that I am your friend? You know I cherish your friendship, and you know I will not violate your confidence. I am, however, human. How much more you can, if you will, trust God by simply believing in Him and in His love and friendship for you."

"I'm beginning to see what you mean," he replied. "I hadn't thought of it in quite that way."

On every side we see the reality of God revealed in nature. We unquestioningly believe the sun will rise each morning and set each evening. We believe the moon will take its appointed place and the stars will follow in their given orbits. We accept without question the orderly succession of the seasons. Yet we ask, "How can I know God? How can I know He really exists? How can I know what He is really like? If God truly is my friend, I need to know Him beyond the visible manifestations in nature."

Yes, you do need to know Him better. Friendship involves sharing, and sharing involves knowing and understanding the nature of our friend.

God — who already knows us, who already knows our needs even before we express them — has, in His infinite love, enabled us to know Him. To know not only His nature, but His desires for us.

"God is our refuge and strength" — but it is through Christ that we come to our full realization of God.

Jesus tells us, "I and My Father are One" — that God, our Father, our friend, acted through Him — that through Him we are to know God and be united with God.

Christ also assures us, "I am the light of the world; he who follows me will not walk in darkness, but will have the light of life" (John 8:12, RSV).

God invites us, "Prove me now . . . if I will not open you the windows of heaven, and pour you out a blessing, that there shall not be room enough to receive it" (Mal. 3:10, KJV).

The way is made clear for us.

God's invitation to prove Him now is clear. (Note the word *invitation*. God is love, and love invites — never intrudes!)

God's promise is clear, for Jesus said, "I assure you that whatever you ask the Father he will give you in my name. Up to now you have asked nothing in my name; ask now, and you will receive, that your joy may be overflowing" (John 16:24, Phillips).

In the giving, receiving, and sharing of human friendship each one of us hopes the relationship will include acknowledgment of our love for our friend, trust in our integrity, and belief in our sincerity. Since, however, these relationships are human and not divine, we are sometimes hurt, disappointed, and disillusioned.

God never, under any circumstances, fails us.

God does not impose upon us all sorts of conditions, restrictions, and rules before He is willing to be our friend.

God does not say, "Stop doing this or that and then I'll talk with you."

God does not say, "Get such and such straightened out and then I'll help you."

Instead, all He asks is that we acknowledge Him, love Him, trust Him, and believe in Him so that He may give to us "that [our] joy may be overflowing."

5
What
Is Prayer?

In light of our Lord's teaching, spiritual life is prayerful communication between ourselves and God.

Prayer, with or without words, is offered to God, and we take our first step to meaningful prayer by our willingness to act.

Prayer is a self-determined, conscious opening of our hearts and minds to God.

It is not the words we use in prayer that are important, for it is possible to use the words of a prayer without really praying at all. In fact, Jesus strongly rebukes mere formalized praying (Matt. 6:5-8; Mark 12:40).

What is important in prayer is our attitude and our intent.

When one of Jesus' disciples said, "Teach us to pray," our Lord answered:

"When ye pray, say,
Our Father [God first]
which art in heaven [God's reign],
Hallowed be thy name [reverence for God].
Thy kingdom come [God's kingdom].
Thy will be done [God's will, not our will]."
(Luke 11:1, 2, KJV)

Then follow our petitions and our needs.

The laws governing prayer are as real, as valid, and as eternal as the laws of nature. And even as man has been left to discover for himself God's laws of nature, so also each of us must discover for ourselves our own vital, personal relationship with God. True, we can be guided by others, but our relationship with God is always personal. And our discovery of this relationship is based upon the law of free will. Our own free will. Our self-determined willingness to act.

Prayer is not a static thing. It involves action. And our willingness to act is based upon our own choice. We alone can resolve this choice into an intention and put the intention into effect.

Jesus rightfully instructs us to put God first. So often we put ourselves first and God second, forgetting Jesus' instruction to us.

Loneliness, grief, pain, depression, fear — all crush the human heart causing anguish and discouragement. Whether or not we intend it, such feelings can take total possession of us. We are absorbed with ourselves. Our hearts are troubled. Yet Jesus instructs us, "Let not your heart be troubled." Here it is important to note the words "your heart."

We can control our hearts if we but remember to put God first. God does not expect us to go it alone."

When we fail to put Him first, we forget to exercise our free will to speak with God who waits to hear us, who does listen, and who does answer.

Here it bears repeating that prayer is a deliberate, directed desire on our part, and our Lord is pledged to listen — for His promises are true and eternal.

In our prayer-conversation with God, listening to Him is an essential part of learning to know Him. How patient God is when so often we insist upon doing all the talking. And when we do this, it is no wonder that our prayers seem stale and rigidly routine — even prayer itself seems more a burden than a blessing.

Prayer always requires more than one. It requires the one who prays and the One who listens.

Jesus did say, "Where two or three are gathered together in my name, there am I in the midst of them" (Matt. 18:20, KJV). But even in group prayer we must never forget our personal one-to-one relationship with God.

Psalm 25:1 (KJV) provides an interesting guide for the direction of our prayers:
"Unto thee, O Lord [God first],
do I [use of our free will]
lift up [our effort]
my soul [the subject of our prayer]."

The psalmist then states his *trust* in God and asks that God *teach* him, *guide* him, *keep* him, and *forgive* him his sins.

Our first prayer is one which reveals our desire and our willingness. What we say in this or in any other prayer is of less importance than our attitude of heart, mind, and will.

God reaches out to us. Through prayer we reach toward Him. Through prayer we are united with Him.

Here, I want to add a postscript to my first chapter:

Jesus said, "*You* also must be ready, because the Son of Man will come at an hour when *you* do not expect him" (Matt. 24:44, NIV).

Our Lord did come at an unexpected hour for Dick, the man in the first chapter who never did pray. Tragically, sadly, and *unnecessarily,* he died alone. Suddenly. Devoid of family and friends. Separated from them and from God by his *own* choice and the exercise of his *own* free will.

6
Be Yourself!

God loves *you*. Loves you for yourself — just as you are and with all the potential you possess.

In our prayer relationship with God it is important that we be ourselves. God does not want, nor expect, us to be otherwise.

We often succeed in fooling others. Sometimes we even fool ourselves. But never, under any circumstances, do we fool God.

If prayer is a new experience for you, and if you still have doubts as to God's reality and His love for you, then it is essential that you make these feelings known in your prayer.

It is also important to keep your prayer language simple, natural, comfortable — to use your own words.

If it is easier for you to pray "God You," instead of "God Thou," then by all means use the more comfortable expression.

If following your first prayer attempt you find yourself tightening up inside — even feeling a bit foolish and then almost resentful — it is critical at this point that you continue to pray and to be honest. That you frankly admit, "Well, God, that's the way I do feel. Please help me to feel Your presence with me. Help me to know You do hear me and will help me."

In this initial prayer, instead of turning from God, you have exercised your free will, and in so doing you have taken your first giant, all-important step toward Him.

God does indeed know exactly how you feel.

God does hear your prayer.

God will help you.

Prayer is sharing. Prayer is caring.

Most people find it helpful to set aside a few minutes a day to be quiet and still, to reflect and to pray. Some find this easier to do in the morning before the day's activities. Others find it easier to do at night. Select for yourself your own quiet time. However, as you grow in your understanding of prayer, you will find yourself, as Paul said, almost "praying without ceasing."

Quick, God-oriented thoughts — too rapid to be formalized into words — can and will become prayers. God speaks to us in many ways. Such quick reactions on our part *are* responses to God speaking to us.

A beloved Christian friend taught me something about prayer I've never forgotten. Let me share it with you.

Lois was a radiant person. Everyone loved her and liked to be with her; they felt comfortable and relaxed in her presence. She made them feel happy, for she was herself a happy person.

People also instinctively knew Lois was close to God. They trusted her and confided in her. They sensed and wanted to share the sustaining inner peace, calm, and assurance she possessed. And none sought her help without receiving it in full, unselfish measure.

I was always intrigued by the warm, wonderful friendship she shared with our Lord. They were on such intimate terms!

One day I saw my friend genuinely amused but sensed something beyond her laughter. I asked about it. She smiled and said, "Well, it was funny, wasn't it? So I just shared it with God." Then she added, "I wonder where people think laughter comes from if not from God?"

If we think about it — why shouldn't we share our mirth with God? Why not indeed? He may even find it a pleasant respite from our usual petitions.

Also, if we think about it — little children were welcomed by our Lord. They wanted to be near Him, with Him. They wanted to touch Him. And I am convinced our Lord not only received these little ones (as we know He did), but that He also smiled with them and laughed with them.

Thinking about this has introduced another dimension to my prayer life. God *is* my friend, and as with any friend, I enjoy sharing my laughter with Him. I can increasingly open my mind to quick prayer thoughts.

Upon waking in the morning I find myself praying, "Good morning, God. Thank You for letting me share with You the beauty of this Your day." For me, this prayer has become as much a happy habit as saying, "Good morning" to any other friend.

You, too, can find ways in which to share with God your daily activities. You will find it helps you get through the most difficult day and even the darkest hours.

Others may fail or disappoint us. God, our friend, *never* fails us.

When asked by a friend how he succeeded in composing such cheerful music for the church, the great composer Franz Joseph Haydn replied:

> I cannot make it otherwise. I write according to the thoughts I feel; when I think upon God, my heart is so full of joy that the notes dance and leap, as it were, from my pen: and since God has given me a cheerful heart, it will be pardoned me that I serve Him with a cheerful spirit.

Modern medicine has established that the patient possessing a cheerful, optimistic, expectant outlook recovers from illness, injury, or surgery far more rapidly than the patient of opposite disposition.

Why?

Because the inner state of our being cannot be separated from our physical selves and has a direct and proportionate bearing on the state of our health.

Repeatedly throughout the Bible God urges us to be "glad," to be "joyful," and to "rejoice."

In Psalm 5:11 (KJV) we read: "Let all those that put their trust in thee rejoice: let them ever shout for joy, because thou defendest them: let them also that love thy name be joyful in thee."

Note in this one verse the words "rejoice," "joy," and "joyful."

In Psalm 9:2 we read, "I will be glad and rejoice in thee: I will sing praise to thy name, O thou most High."

In Psalm 16:9 we read, "My heart is glad, and my glory rejoiceth."

In Psalm 100:2 we are instructed how we shall ally ourselves with God. "Serve the Lord with gladness."

It is impossible to give genuine expression to "joy," "rejoicing," "being glad," or "gladness" if we are bogged down with fear, hate, and resentment, or are enshrouded in sorrow on the brink of despair.

You may be saying, "How can you write about rejoicing when I find nothing in which to rejoice? How can you write about being glad when I am so unhappy?"

Let me ask you something.

Has any sorrowful, unhappy, despairing person you know ever helped rid you of all that depresses you? I doubt it. In fact, most of us find ourselves uncomfortable or thrust into even deeper gloom in the presence of such people.

A woman I know permitted her faith in God to be overruled by her dislike of her new son-in-law. She let her opinion cloud the previously harmonious love shared with her daughter. Resentments took root in her and grew until they strangled her with bitterness and destroyed the rapport she had enjoyed with the rest of her family. Then when she suddenly lost her husband, all memories of joy and happiness she had known with him were obliterated by negative thoughts she permitted to intrude upon her consciousness. When her daughter died, this woman's bitterness and resentment multiplied as did her loneliness and despair. She shunned all who truly wished to help and permitted in her presence only those who further commiserated with her in her own self-imposed gloom.

Note carefully that I said this woman *permitted* her faith to be overruled by her own thoughts.

Note that I said she *permitted* her own judgment to destroy harmony within herself and with others.

Her own resentments impaired her health.

Her own actions excluded others from her life.

God had not in any way failed her.

It was she who permitted all these factors to shut God out of her life and out of her thoughts.

In tribute to this same woman, let me add that she has, of her own free will, returned to the earlier faith she knew. In so doing she found our Lord patiently waiting.

God never intrudes.

Jesus said, "Behold, I stand at the door and knock." He does *not* batter down the door! Instead, He gently raps. A reminder that He is there, courteously awaiting our invitation to let Him enter our lives.

Whether the Lord awaits our opening of the door for the first time — or whether He awaits the reopening of the door we have closed — He *always* leaves the decision to us.

If you were to say to the woman previously mentioned, "But I just can't open (or reopen) the door of my heart. I'm too old. Too much has happened," she would reply, "Nonsense! As long as we live it is *never* too late! Just don't continue to ignore God's invitation as I did until I was in my eighties. You may not live to be my age."

R. W. Dale once said, "We ask God to forgive us our evil thoughts and evil temper, but rarely, if ever, ask Him to forgive us our sadness."

If you are oppressed by sorrows, if your thoughts are those of despair, if your mind harbors resentments and fears, if your life seems devoid of happiness, and joy has become a stranger — then your first prayer need is for love. God's love. God's understanding. God's forgiveness. God's restorative power to bring peace and happiness back into your life. His blessing of light to flood the darkest crevices of gloom in your mind. You need to let Him sweep away the cobwebs of doubt which plague you. The dust of despair which clings to the garments of your thoughts.

Be still for a moment. Be quiet. Silence your clamorous thoughts. Open the door of your mind and heart.

God does not demand that you fling open all the inner doors and windows of yourself at once. He *never* requires more than you are capable of giving at any one time. He does, however, ask you to "be still" and to be quiet so that you may "know Him."

Open your heart and thoughts and in your own words pray, "Oh, God, please enter my thoughts with the light of Your love for me. Cleanse me of despair. Wipe away my doubts. Sweep away my selfish gloom. Help me to know and feel Your abiding presence. Help me to believe and understand that You will fill the emptiness and needs of my life in accordance with my faith to let You do so. Thank You for hearing me and for even now answering my prayer. Help me to be quiet. To listen. To know You are my friend."

7

You Are Unique!

How often we hear the cry of anger or despair: "Why does God do this?" Or, "Why did God let this happen?"

Such questions arise from a wrong concept of God and imply that God is not loving. That He is not wise. That He is not good.

If we are to know God and know Him as our friend, we must first know that He loves us.

We must know that when we use the pronoun *I* we mean by it someone unique, special, and consciously distinct from any other person — ever.

My mind is my own. If I think, it is because I choose to think.

My free will is my own.

My spirit (made in the image of God) is my personal spirit. It belongs to me and to no one else.

My conscious willingness to know God is dictated by my mind and involves my personal relationship with Him.

Only through a full realization and awareness of who I am — a child of God, and as such I am unique — can I discover my personal relationship with Him. Only then can I hope to truly converse with God through prayer — whether through prayer offered alone or with others.

God is my God and my friend.
God is also your God and your friend.
He is our God and our friend.

Christ is my personal Savior.
Christ is (or can be) your personal Savior.
He is our Savior.

Each of us is not only unique but uniquely alone.
Alone, we are born.
Alone, we commit ourselves to marriage or remaining single.
Alone, we confess Christ as our personal Savior.
Alone, we are baptized.
Alone, we shall die.
Alone, we shall be buried.
Alone, we shall be judged by our Savior — to whom God has committed such judgment.
Alone, we shall be absolved of sin through our personal Savior, Jesus Christ.

Someone once asked Daniel Webster, "What is the most important thought you have ever had?" He replied, "My individual responsibility to God."

It is impossible for anyone else to lift up my living soul to my living God.

Others may pray with me or pray for me, but my individual responsibility to God remains my own. No one can do my praying, just as no one can do my living — except me.

And no one can repent for me.

Nor can anyone else be forgiven my sins.

Unless I, who am uniquely myself, consciously exercise my desire and my free will to pray, then I, by choice, remain out of touch with God.

Only when I do exercise my unique free will to know God am I no longer alone in my unique aloneness.

Rosalind Rinker in her book *Communicating Love Through Prayer* says:

> How can we love ourselves, until we are certain that God loves us? But when we know that He does indeed love us, then everything changes! Then we can tell it, and others listening will believe us, because they know we are speaking from the heart and from personal experience.[1]

When we *know* God loves us, it is a wonderful, personal, unique experience. Things do change for us. We no longer have to feel alone because we are no longer alone.

Others listening to us believe us because we speak

[1]Rosalind Rinker, *Communicating Love Through Prayer* (Grand Rapids: Zondervan Publishing House, 1966), p. 15.

the truth born from an in-depth, unique, heart-mind, personal experience.

Ros Rinker says;

> Christ's life on earth revealed His love and mercy and kindness for people who had lost their way and knew it. His severity was for those false at heart.[2]

In "unique aloneness" many do lose their way. But God our friend, through Christ, stands at the door of our heart and consciousness with His gift of love.

You are unique.

Are you still alone?

8
Permitting and Daring

If we permit our thoughts to become narrow, cramped, and stifled, we do not live — we merely exist.

If we permit our thoughts to get into a rut, life becomes dull and uninteresting — and so do we.

If we permit such thoughts to dominate our lives, then our faith, our sympathies, and our prayers are out of harmony with God — and we are out of harmony with ourselves.

Equally important is what we permit ourselves to think about prayer. What we think prayer is. What we think it should be. How we think prayer should be "prayed."

I suspect many people refrain from praying because they permit themselves to think of prayer as a restrictive experience having a set of rigid rules.

If in our prayer life we permit, or insist upon, limiting our prayer by a repetition of the same words (makes for dull conversation), holding the same narrow views (precludes growth), using always the same prayer methods (shows we are in a rut), we shall never really learn how to expand our prayer life. And we shall never discover how rich, how varied in expression, our prayers can be.

Prayer should be — can be — a forceful, dynamic experience! Can be, if we permit ourselves to remember it is an experience between our unique living soul and our living God and friend.

When we remember this, our prayers will be filled with expectancy and exploration.

Our prayer life should be — can be — a wonderful, ever-expanding adventure in love and in friendship with God.

In our prayer life we should feel — can feel — a real sense of space, length, breadth, depth, height, and growth — all felt through freedom. Freedom to love God and to know we are loved by Him.

In prayer, we also need to permit ourselves a sense of daring.

Daring to trust God. All the way. In everything.

Daring to explore with Him the unlimited boundaries of His love and concern for us. For our unique living souls.

Daring to intrepidly climb spiritual mountains.

Daring to pause for rest and catch our spiritual breath.

Daring to be quiet beside the still waters.

Daring to walk leisurely in the green pastures knowing God our friend walks with us.

Daring to permit wonderful, extemporaneous prayers to be part of our prayer life. Spontaneous prayers that spring suddenly and effortlessly from our hearts. Unpremeditated prayers specially offered to God our friend.

Daring before many of our prayers to decide, as a matter of courteous communication, just what it is we wish to pray about. Remembering that conversation requires listening as well as speaking.

Daring to remember that the number of our prayers is not important.

Daring to remember that the rhetoric of our prayers is not important.

Daring to remember that the eloquence of our prayers is not important.

Daring to remember that the length of our prayers is not important.

Daring to remember that the logic and the method of our prayers are not important.

Daring to ask God our friend to help us forget all that prayer is not — that we may know instead what prayer really is.

Daring to ask God our friend to help us remember that it is always our desire and sincerity in prayer which really count.

Daring to permit God's love to enter our lives and change them.

9

Where Do

You Abide?

Jesus began His ministry on earth by a retreat. By being still. By being quiet.

In the solitude of the wilderness, in prayerful communication with God, He gathered strength and found the courage and power to do the work God sent Him to do.

As stated earlier, Jesus strongly rebuked mere formalized praying. Our Lord does, however, set an example for us by the manner in which He conducted His prayer life.

He arose early and sought a solitary place; there, quietly alone, He prayed (Mark 1:35).

Jesus was praying when the Holy Spirit came to Him at His baptism (Luke 3:21).

After the miracle of the feeding of the five thousand, Jesus "went up into a mountain apart to pray: and when the evening was come, he was there alone" (Matt. 14:23, KJV).

Before choosing His twelve disciples, Jesus "went out into a mountain to pray, and continued all night in prayer to God" (Luke 6:12, KJV).

In the Gospel of Luke we learn that at the time of the transfiguration Jesus was praying (Luke 9:28, 29).

Jesus' complete intimacy with God the Father is revealed in His prayer of intercession (John 17).

Prayer carried our Lord through Gethsemane where He prayed in agony (Luke 22:41-44).

And Jesus' last words on the cross were a prayer. He entered heaven praying, "Father, into your hands I commit my spirit" (Luke 23:46, NIV).

By drawing apart for a period of quietude — alone with God — we, too, can gain strength and courage to do our work and to resist and repel the temptations which are disruptive, damaging, and destructive.

We know our Lord was tempted (Matt. 4). We also know that Jesus knew the source of such temptation, and we know the defense He used to resist it and win.

Jesus conquered both sin and death.

When we are tempted (and we all are), when we are fearful, it is Christ who is our defense. It is Christ who is our way to victory.

I have an attractive neighbor who more than once has said, "I'll never be good enough to win God's approval. I'm afraid I'll go to hell."

She does not mean this facetiously. She really is afraid, and her fears have overlapped into other areas of her life. She wants to do creative things and has the intelligence and ability to do them, but she is afraid to start for fear she will fail. As she continues to postpone taking positive action, her migraine headaches increase in painful proportion.

Jesus healed those who were sad, lonely, and despairing. He healed those who were broken in body, mind, or spirit. He cleansed those who sinned. He healed the brokenhearted. And He healed those whose lives were cramped by fear and doubt.

His are the gifts of hope, of joy, and of life — life eternal.

Christ's love brought hope to the most despairing heart. His love still does.

The life and the love of our Lord show us what God the Father is — love.

Rosalind Rinker says:

> Many believe they know what Jesus looks like. Others do not. The important thing, here and now, is not what Jesus looked like while on earth, but whether we are aware of His Presence with us. . . . The reality of Jesus' presence is not reserved for a favored few, unless you call the "favored few" those who seek Him.[1]

Jesus tells us, "If you abide in me, and my words abide in you, ask whatever you will, and it shall be done unto you" (John 15:7, RSV).

To abide means to remain — permanently — not just spend a day or a night as a traveler does.

[1]Rinker, *Communicating Love*, pp. 99,100.

To abide in Christ means we believe in the living Christ. To believe in the living Christ means we can accept His promise that He will help us conquer our problems, our fears, and our doubts. And through Him, who has conquered sin and death itself, we have everlasting life.

Where do you abide?

so that your Father also who is in heaven may forgive you your trespasses" (Mark 11:22-25, RSV).

The key words in what our Lord says bear repeating: "does not doubt," "believe," "forgive." In these three areas each of us can use God's continuing help.

We cannot expect our prayers to be answered if we approach them as did a woman who, having heard these words of Jesus from a friend, closed her eyes and prayed, "Lord, You know the hill just beyond my window which obstructs my view. I now say to this hill, 'Get up and throw yourself into the sea,' Amen." She opened her eyes, looked out the window, sighed, and said to herself, "Oh, well, I knew it would still be there anyway."

If we feel half-hearted about God, our spiritual pulse is weak and so are our prayers.

If our love for God is an intermittent — on again, off again — sort of relationship, then this irregularity and vacillation will be reflected in our prayer communication.

If we are tempted to say, "I forgot to pray," we deceive ourselves. It is not that we forgot to pray — we forgot God. But He does not forget us.

If prayer does not interest us, then we are not interested in God. God, however, is interested in us.

If to us prayer does not seem to be real communication, then it is because God is not real to us. But we are real to Him for He created us.

In our hearts we know whether we pray because we really want to pray, or whether we pray from habit, or whether we pray because we are afraid not to pray. We know the difference and so does God.

If we have permitted any of these negative aspects to clog our channels of prayer communication, then we need to be healed and free of them.

Jesus said, "They that are whole need not a physician" (Luke 5:31, KJV), but when we do need healing Jesus assures us that "the prayer of faith shall save the sick, and shall raise him up" (James 5:15, KJV).

According to many doctors, negative attitudes account for at least 50 percent of our physical ills. Some authorities place the percentage as high as 85 percent.

What we think, then, does have a direct and inescapable bearing on the state of our spiritual, mental, and physical well-being.

If our minds are burdened with bitter, angry, resentful, unforgiving thoughts, our bodies react. Sooner or later, these negative thoughts will manifest themselves in a variety of unwanted ways. We need healing. We need the healing of the Great Physician. The healing of Jesus Christ.

If doubts and fears nibble at the edges of our thoughts, we need healing. If we are sad, lonely, on the brink of despair, we need healing.

Often we fail to connect the splitting headache, the upset stomach, overeating, indigestion, irritability, and sleepless nights with our emotions. Especially so if we pride ourselves on our outward control of anger, displeasure, or hurt feelings.

On the surface we may appear to have controlled such feelings and emotions. In reality we have only succeeded in thrusting them damagingly deeper into the depths of our inner selves.

Another common self-deceptive technique we employ is that of rationalization to excuse our feelings and our behavior. We blame someone else or something else. We disguise our feelings to such an extent that we can no longer recognize them for what they really are. We need our Lord's cleansing and healing of our unconscious minds, that we may consciously cooperate with Him in restoring our spiritual health.

To ourselves, we are important. We are, however, much more important to God, for He loves us. Our living souls return to Him.

Since God did create us, and since He does love us, He knows that just as our physical bodies need nourishment and exercise, so do our spiritual selves.

None of us, however independent we like to think ourselves, are totally self-sufficient. We do need others. And each of us wants and needs love, acceptance, and approval. To protest otherwise is self-delusion.

It has been medically established that infants have died not from lack of food, but from lack of personal, human touch. Lack of physical and emotional affection. Lack of being held close. Lack of feeling loved and wanted.

The need to be loved, to be wanted, is inherent in each of us.

When we feel we are not loved, not wanted, not needed, all sorts of troubles begin, and often the result is our not being able to love even ourselves.

If for you prayer is a new experience, you will, in effect, be asking for healing — the healing of God's presence with you. The healing knowledge that God loves you. That God hears you. That He understands you and is responding to your needs.

If you are returning to prayer, then it is with a desire for God's healing of your weary soul which has journeyed far over rough paths and needs rest.

If you already pray, you still need God's help to keep your spiritual life and prayer communication vital, alert, interesting, and healthy.

It has been wisely said that "one with God constitute a majority." *Know* this. *Believe* this — for it is true.

God does hear your prayer, and it will be answered. Perhaps answered sooner, or later, than you expected. Or answered in a way other than you expected. But your prayer, if sincere, will be answered. *Believe* this.

Try praying for someone else. It will bring a whole new dimension into your prayer communication — a new sense of direction, clarity, and understanding.

It is truly in giving that we receive.

11
Learning More About God

If we are to make our prayer communication a wonderful and growing adventure, then we need a deeper knowledge of God, our friend, and of Christ, our Savior and our friend.

Initially we do this in the same way we come to know people: By being with them. By thinking of them. By hearing others speak of them. By reading letters from them. And by our desire to increasingly know them better. It is in all of these ways and more that our acquaintances become our friends.

Most of us have many acquaintances — few real friends. Friendship involves a *willing* responsibility.

A *will*ingness to give of ourselves. A *will*ingness to care and to be genuinely concerned for the welfare and the happiness of our friend. A *will*ingness to share. A *will*ingness to devote time to our friend. A *will*ingness to listen to our friend. A *will*ingness to know the quiet moment with our friend when there is no need for words. The moment when hearts speak the silent language of love.

It is in similar ways that we gradually come to know and trust God.

We can, if we *will*, learn more about God through His living Word, the Bible.

We can learn more about God by talking with others who already know Him. And by seeking a united fellowship with Him in the community of other Christians.

As our desire to seek and know God increases, He will increasingly reveal Himself to us — in many ways. And with each prayer step we will find new encouragement to take the next step until we truly are able to walk with Him.

As we learn to walk in trust with God, we begin to realize what is meant by the grace of God. For it is by God's grace that we continually receive His love. And our assurance that we do continually receive this love is fully disclosed to us by Jesus Christ, who is Himself the sacrificial expression of the grace of God.

To be in a "state of grace" means we realize our relationship with God is not accomplished by our own goodness nor by our own merits but only by our faith in Christ who reveals God's merciful love to us and His gift of salvation for us.

If we forget that grace is the power of God, then our prayers may become stale and we will not feel spiritually refreshed.

The power of God's grace can work within us (Eph. 3:20), but it requires our cooperation through prayer. Without this gift of grace we cannot truly pray, for it is a power that comes to us from God Himself.

It is this special and individual gift of grace coming into our souls that enables us to communicate with our living God and Savior.

It is this gift of grace which enables us to *know* God, and as we do to truly and joyfully lift up our hearts to the Lord our God in prayer.

12
God's Word

God's Word,[1] the Bible, has been translated into more languages than any other book in the world. Each year millions of copies are sold. Millions of copies are presented as gifts. Copies are found in hotels and motels in all fifty states. Nearly every home contains at least one copy. Nearly everyone seems ready to discuss or debate this Book of books.

[1]Author's note: As mentioned in the previous chapter, God's living Word is the Bible. It constitutes an extremely important and vital link in our knowledge of, and relationship with, God our friend.

This particular chapter differs from those which precede it and those which follow it. I have, however, intentionally inserted it at this point with the hope that it will provide both insight and incentive for readers not yet familiar with this remarkable Book of books.

How many actually read it or understand it is another question.

"All too many Christians," says a clergyman friend of mine, "seem content to maintain no more than a fourth-grade level of spiritual education when it comes to a knowledge of their Christian beliefs. Many," he continues sadly, "resented my saying this in one of my sermons when I admonished them for not according the same effort of study to the Bible as they do to other subjects."

Not long ago I talked with an Air Force Navigator who is a member of a large Protestant denomination. He stated that he has a Bible in his home but admitted he has never read it. He then hastily added, "But I always carry a copy of the New Testament in a pocket of my flight suit."

"Why," I asked, "if you never bother to read it?"

"I don't know," was his honest reply.

"Someday why don't you take a look at the New Testament Book of James?" I suggested, "You may find it interesting."

Looking slightly puzzled, he asked, "Why that particular book?"

I smiled, "Because," I replied, "it is short, practical, and to the point. It may encourage you as a Christian to read more."

As Sir Walter Scott lay dying, he asked that his friend Lockhart read to him from "the Book."

"What book?" asked his friend.

"There is but one Book," was the reply.

Earlier Scott had written:

The most learned, acute, and diligent student cannot, in the longest life, obtain an entire knowledge of this one volume. The more deeply he works the mine, the richer and more abundant he finds the ore; new light continually beams from this source of heavenly knowledge, to direct the conduct, and illustrate the work of God and the ways of men; and he will at last leave the world confessing, that the more he studied the Scriptures, the fuller conviction he had of his own ignorance, and of their inestimable value.[2]

The English clergyman James Hamilton wrote,

The Word of God will stand a thousand readings; and he who has gone over it the most frequently is the surest of finding new wonders there.[3]

Renowned scientists, philosophers, scholars, and statesmen place the Bible above all other literature.

Shakespeare makes literally hundreds of references and allusions to the Bible.

Leonardo da Vinci and Michelangelo both drew inspiration from the Bible as have other world-famous artists, sculptors, writers, essayists, and poets.

What sort of volume, then, is this Bible which has led people of all stations in life to seek guidance, inspiration, and solace from its pages?

Actually, the Bible is a library within itself since it contains many books. Within these books we find, as Dr. James L. Vance has so eloquently summarized:

History, poetry, prophecy, theology, oratory, humor, sarcasm, irony, music, drama, tragedy, strategy, love tales, war tales, travelogues, laws, jurisprudence, songs, sermons, warnings, prayers . . . . Was there ever such literature? The Bible begins

[2]Tryon Edwards, ed., *New Dictionary of Thoughts* (New York: Standard Book Company, 1955).

[3]Ibid.

with a garden and ends with a city. It starts with a morning followed by a night, and ends with a day that shall know no night. It breaks the silence with, "In the beginning God," and it hushes the universe to sleep with, "The grace of our Lord Jesus Christ be with you all." It finds man at the shut gates of the lost Eden, and leaves him before the open door at the top of the road.[4]

If you have never read the Bible, or have for some reason long neglected it, I would like to suggest *The Gospels* — the four Gospels translated into modern English by J. B. Phillips. It provides a superbly readable version of the passages that are the very essence of Christianity.

The Revised Standard Version of the Bible, containing both the Old and New Testaments, translates into modern language biblical words and phrases which have become obscured by time and have consequently lost their meaning, or for one reason or another are no longer clear. This Revised Standard Version is an authorized version of the American Standard Version, published in 1901, which was a revision of the familiar King James Version, published in 1611.

A popular contemporary paraphrase of the Bible is *The Living Bible,* available in several formats.

Many excellent translations are available in both hardcover and paperback. But regardless of which translation or paraphrase you choose, I urge you to start your reading with the Gospels.

Dr. Edgar J. Goodspeed recommends reading the Gospel of Mark first and in its entirety. This can be

[4]Source unknown.

done easily in less than one hour. By following the Gospel of Mark with that of Matthew you retain continuity, for the Gospel of Matthew is in essence an expansion of Mark. In Matthew the teachings of our Lord appear in a series of six sermons. In the first, the Sermon on the Mount, Jesus gives us the most comprehensive statement of Christian ethics ever made. Here also we find the Beatitudes, the Golden Rule, and the Lord's Prayer.

Like Matthew, Luke makes extensive use of the earlier Gospel of Mark. The careful phrasing and style used by Luke reveal him as a reliable historian. However, it is the manner in which Luke portrays the deep love, sympathy, and compassion of Jesus which helps us understand why the apostle Paul called Luke "the beloved physician." With unusual gentleness and understanding this Gospel embraces all races and conditions; it is also the Gospel of hope for those who have sinned and failed.

Although it is possible that John, the author of the fourth Gospel, knew both Mark and Luke, biblical scholars believe it is less probable that he knew Matthew, for John writes in a style uniquely his own. This Gospel is frequently regarded as inspired meditation upon the life of Jesus and the significance of the Divinity with the humanity in Christ (the Incarnation).

A study of the Gospels enables us to read with greater compassion and understanding about the people and the events which are so vividly portrayed in the books of the Old Testament.

The psalms of the Old Testament speak to the universal heart of mankind, for they contain a complete record of human emotions. In them we read of love and hate, hope and despair, sorrow and delight, confession of sin and joy in forgiveness.

The sententious sayings found in the Old Testament Book of Proverbs presents Hebrew wisdom in its most distinctive form. In these proverbs we read of anger, pride, falsehood, envy, avarice, ignorance, and folly. Conversely, we read of knowledge, truth, tact, generosity, cheerfulness, mercy, reverence, and understanding.

Stanley Baldwin wrote:

The Holy Bible is not only great but highly explosive literature. It works in strange ways and no living man can tell or know how that book in its journeyings through the world has started an individual soul 10,000 different places into a new life, a new belief, a new conception and a new faith.

In the course of even the busiest day, most of us find time to read the newspaper, glance at our favorite magazine, watch the television program of our choice — but rationalize about not having time to read the Bible.

Does it really make sense that we should be eager to keep abreast with current events and drag our feet when it comes to information about the gospel, which is the *best news* that has ever been reported in the history of the world?

The Bible is the only book that gives certain knowledge of the future. It is the only book that satisfactorily answers the questions:

Where did I come from?

Why am I here?

Where am I going?

13
How Do
You See Things?

Some who read this book will find it too liberal — others too fundamental. Individual viewpoints will of course be contingent upon individual experience. Our lives are marked by what we have seen, heard, and experienced.

How we continue to see things influences what we believe. And what we believe has a direct bearing upon our entire lives which includes our spiritual lives.

Many do see spiritual matters as something to be blotted out of their lives. Such faulty vision may be the result of any one of a number of things. Let us examine a few.

Often we hear the old cliché, "I never argue religion or politics."

I find the lumping together of religion and politics rather curious, for the first pertains to our belief (or non-belief) in God and to our relationship with Him. Politics has to do with political parties and the management of public policy. Further, politics — in the negative sense — means dishonest management to secure the success of political candidates or parties.

We may mismanage our own lives, and others may employ mismanagement or dishonest means to secure their own success or the success of others, but God our friend never resorts to such tactics.

However, there may sometimes be a certain validity for the expression, "I never argue religion or politics."

In the colloquial sense, to argue religion or politics implies that people get into fights rather than discussions. Especially since few are skilled in the art of polemics or the practice of disputation or debate.

Sadly, many adults do use this expression because as children they have witnessed their elders in heated disputes over religion, or politics, or both, and as adults they seek to tune out all discussion on either subject.

Another adult cliché is, "If I were to enter a church, the church would fall down." While this remark is meant to be facetious, it does imply the height of misguided self-conceit.

Some adults retain unpleasant childhood memories which include having been forced in the name of religion to do and to witness things they found not only distasteful but frightening. Having been "religiously" coerced and threatened as children, it is no wonder many adults harbor a cold disdain for "religion" and find it a subject to be assiduously avoided.

Still other adults are quick to point out hypocrites within the "church," thereby finding a self-righteous excuse for their own nonchurch affiliation.

God our friend knows those whose hearts, intentions, and actions are hypocritical. They are unsuccessfully trying to imitate something of inestimable value. I doubt that there ever was a hypocrite who expended time and energy trying to imitate that which was worthless.

If you happen to use any or all of the above hackneyed expressions, then this book is written especially for you. It is especially you I invite to further consideration and exploration of your potential for true and lasting friendship with God.

In 1 Corinthians 13:11 (NIV) we read:

"When I was a child, I talked like a child, I thought like a child, I reasoned like a child. When I became a man, I put childish ways behind me."

It appears we often succeed in putting away childish ideas and notions in every respect except those which relate to God and our relationship with Him.

The word *empathy* is a special word, for it means a peculiarly intimate understanding — an ability, so to speak, to put yourself in another's shoes.

If you have been turned-off by spiritual matters, I am convinced it has not been without reason. If I knew your reason for feeling as you do, I could not help but empathize with you. Yet I'm sure you will not fault me for wanting to again invite you to discover for yourself that God is your friend.

You can reverse a negative course of thinking and make it a positive course of action.

I urge you to make explorative efforts that are expansive as well as hopeful and expectant.

In prayer we turn to God in order that through Him — through Christ — we may ourselves be changed. Changed in our perspective. Changed in how we view ourselves and others.

If we truly wish to have 20/20 spiritual vision, then we must be willing to recognize that there is only one source — God — who can correct the "blind spots" in our lives and in our thinking.

Jesus Himself cautions us in this respect, for in reply to the rich man who addressed Him as "Good Teacher," Jesus said, "Why do you call me good? No one is good but God alone" (Mark 10:18, RSV).

If you do not yet know Christ, the Gospel of Mark is especially important for it reveals our Savior to us in human terms we sometimes forget. This Gospel tells us about Jesus eating (2:15,16; 14:3, RSV), drinking (2:16, KJV), being weary and needing sleep (4:38, RSV), becoming angry (3:5, RSV), showing wonder or astonishment (6:6, RSV), becoming indignant (10:14, RSV), being greatly troubled and distressed (14:33, RSV), and even feeling forsaken (15:34, RSV). In this same Gospel, Jesus' personal touch is frequently mentioned as is His compassion and mercy for others (5:19, RSV) plus His love for others (10:21, RSV).

Throughout His entire ministry, Jesus always glorified God and clearly said that He spoke not on His own authority, but only on God's authority, and that it was God who worked through Him.

God can and will work through you. He can and will help you to *see* yourself and others and all things with a new and refreshing clarity.

God is your friend.

All He asks of you is your willingness to cooperate with Him by keeping your prayers as an open channel through which communication becomes a reality.

14
God's Invitation

Within each one of us is an inescapable longing. A longing peculiarly our own. Uniquely our own. A longing especially prevalent in our solitary moments. Sometimes fleetingly. Sometimes more insistently. It is God's invitation to know Him. It is an invitation which must, sooner or later, be answered. Answered by either acceptance or rejection.

As Helen Keller so beautifully described it, this inner longing is an "inherited capacity — a sort of sixth sense — a soul sense which sees, hears, feels, all in one."

If you have already accepted God's invitation, then you have already resolved this longing.

If you stand on the threshold of decision, you know the decision must be your own. God does not intrude. He invites.

An eminently successful businessman, Dr. Samuel M. Best, once stood — perhaps like yourself — at the gate of decision. He wrote that in his private moments of mental inventory, he discovered he had no more peace of mind, nor was he less afraid of the problems of life and death, than many years before when he planned his road to happiness and success. The reason for his continued unrest and fear was that he had neglected spiritual values in his anxiety for material gain.

If in your own planning you have excluded God, then you will find, as someone said, that you "haven't that within you which is above you — and you will soon yield to that which is around you." A feeling of emptiness will shadow even the brightest moments of your self-confidence, for something is still missing. God is missing.

We cannot, no matter how we try, banish the thought of God from our lives. The more we try to do so, the more God returns to our thoughts.

When only a lad of nine years, Chateauneuf, who became keeper of the seals for Louis XIII, was questioned by a bishop about his beliefs. One day the prelate said, "I will give you an orange if you will tell me where God is." "My lord," answered the boy, "I will give you two oranges if you will tell me where He is not."

We can no more escape God than we can escape breathing. While we live, God seeks quietly, gently, persuasively to enter our lives. To become part of us. To become our beloved friend.

Years ago when Edwin Booth, the famous actor, was at the height of his fame, he received a letter from a clergyman anxious to see his performance. At the time, many considered it sinful to attend theatrical performances. The minister requested that Mr. Booth permit him to enter the theater by a private door as he did not wish any who knew him to see him entering such a place. "Sir," replied Booth, "there is no door in my theater through which God cannot see."

In our lives, there is no door through which God does not see. But remember, God, who is love, always sees us with compassion and understanding.

Is your life self-centered? Or is it God-centered?

How have you responded to the Lord's invitation?

If you are still hesitating, still debating — then the question put daily to Lee Bristol as a child by his mother is worth your consideration: "Has your soul grown today?"

15
When You
Accept

Acceptance of the Lord's invitation brings with it many wonderful changes in our lives and our thinking.

When we love someone and are proud of them, it is natural to want the joy of introducing them to, and sharing them with, others.

Christians are always proud to introduce their Savior to those who do not know Him. But the results of this introduction, regardless of how sincere, are contingent upon how it is done.

We who are Christians cannot hope to reach others if we have permitted deterioration in our own faith. If our faith has become weak, narrow, or restricted, then we, ourselves, need spiritual healing.

As Christians, it is well for us to remember we have all sinned. So have others. The only difference is that we have the blessed assurance born of faith that our sins will be forgiven.

As Christians, we are sometimes confronted by those who are eager to cite our past or present errors. This can prove embarrassing or humiliating. But it need not. If we have been honest with ourselves and with God, we can then be honest with others. We can then witness for our Savior and emerge from any confrontation spiritually strengthened and with greater love, compassion, and understanding for others.

We don't like to have anything crammed down our throats. We dislike domineering persons intent upon proving themselves right and us totally wrong. So when we do witness for our Lord, let us try to remember that gently *suggesting* accomplishes far more than stubbornly *imposing.* And that it *is* possible to *disagree* without being *disagreeable.*

Love is the language of the heart, not of the head. Let us try to let love do the talking and let love's actions speak for themselves.

In any effort to share our faith, let us remember the admonition of James in the New Testament, "The tongue is a little member and boasts of great things" (James 3:5, RSV). Our tongues, unless curbed, can sometimes do more harm than good in our efforts to witness. Doubly so, if we permit impatience or intolerance to betray us into rudeness.

In our desire to introduce our Lord, let us remember His ministry. Jesus' purpose was to bring God to *all* men and women — not just a select few. He mingled with all sorts of people in all sorts of places. He attended dinners and gatherings. His first recorded miracle is that of turning water into wine at a wedding celebration to which He had been invited. He talked with men and women from the highest to the lowest stations in life. He met with them on quiet mountainsides and in the hearts of busy cities. When He spoke to people of the soil, He spoke in terms they understood. He captured their immediate attention as One familiar with their particular problems and needs.

Whether speaking to theologians, lawyers, politicians, housewives, rulers, or fishermen — rich or poor — Jesus always spoke simply and directly to them in terms they readily understood.

Christians reach people by mingling and sharing with them — for the easiest way to keep our faith is to "give it away."

Most important of all — when we do witness for our Lord, let us not forget that He said:

"I am the vine, *you* are the branches. He who abides in me and I in him, he it is that bears much fruit, for apart from me *you* can do nothing" (John 15:5, RSV).